The MAGIC of C

PA

Celia Shute

Published by The British Porcelain Artist

Westfield House, North Avenue,
Wakefield, W. Yorkshire,
WF1 3RX. England.
Copyright Celia Shute.

British Library Cataloguing-in-Publication Data.
A catalogue record for this book is available from the British Library.
Shute, Celia
The Magic of China Painting.
Porcelain and china painting.

ISBN.
0-9520517-0-2

Whenever you've painted something well you really feel a tremendous excitement. The magic moment is when you open the kiln door and there's your piece of china, glowing and shining, waiting for you to pick it up and experience the thrill of holding your own hand painted china.

Many magic moments come from all the wonderful friends you will make at classes, seminars, demonstrations and conventions. All these things contribute to the 'magic' that is china painting.

During the years that I have been china painting I have made numerous friends throughout the china painting world. I have been very fortunate to watch many talented china painters at work and have received plenty of encouragement with my own china painting.

This book is my way of passing on some help and advice to new china painters and perhaps those a little more advanced. Spreading the magic further afield. Even as I write this down, more and more ideas and techniques come along in china painting; hopefully "The British Porcelain Artist Magazine" which is produced at Westfield House will keep everyone up to date and in touch with new ideas as they come along.

Celia Shute.

For more information about "The British Porcelain Artist", a bi-monthly china painting magazine write to: Westfield House, North Avenue, Wakefield, West Yorkshire, WF1 3RX, England.

CONTENTS

IN THE BEGINNING.

Was there a time before china painting ? This is the question my husband often asks!
People ask me what I did before I started china painting, well I think I've tried every craft that has ever been invented; Gemini people are known for trying lots of different things and notorious for having many things started and nothing finished, so in that respect I'm a typical Gemini. In the past I've done Macrame, Batik, tailoring, made lampshades, candle making, producing plaster cast bears and painting them, sticking together plastic kits of sailing ships, I even tried water colour painting, but after several weeks of trying to paint over some bright red paper the tutor was trying to use up, I decided watercolour painting was not for me.

Then one day I saw some beautiful hand painted plates at a craft fair in Harrogate. The artist was away at lunch, so I waited anxiously for her return. I had always admired nice pieces of china, but hadn't realised that anyone could hand paint china.

At last the artist returned and of course I couldn't wait to ask if she gave lessons. Wonderful, she did, twice a week at her home. "Could I join?" I asked. "Oh yes we'd be delighted to have someone else join our small group", she said. She was amazed when I gave her my address, imagine I was actually going to drive from Wakefield to Harrogate for a china painting lesson! (Approximately one and a half hours drive).

Monday mornings were a hectic time, rushing round getting the 'chores' done, then rushing off to Harrogate for my lessons. I will always remember the patience, kindness and encouragement given to me by Flo Wood, my china painting teacher and the friendliness of my fellow students. That was it , I was hooked. I was absolutely obsessed to learn to paint well. I still have my first efforts and they remind me of how hard it was to get anything onto those slick surfaces, but determination won through, this was one hobby I was not going to give up.

One lesson a week wasn't enough, so I joined Flo's other class on Wednesday evenings, inbetween I painted whenever I had some spare time. Practice, practice, practice.

When I first started china painting, my family had looked on good humouredly. They thought it was just my latest hobby. My husband was working hard with his business and my son Glen was 18 doing 'A' Levels and my daughter Jan, aged 15 was fully occupied with her 'O' Level studies. Jan and I used to share our large kitchen table in the evenings, me with my painting 'stuff' and her with her homework.

It had been September when I started at my china painting class, as Xmas came nearer I wondered if my husband Peter might think a kiln would make a suitable Xmas present. I was so obsessed with my new hobby I just couldn't think of being without a kiln to do my own firing.

My teacher was only too happy to advise me on what to buy. At that time there weren't many top loading kilns in the U.K. (1979), so I had to buy a small pottery kiln which was very well made and will last me forever.

Well, my kiln arrived and was installed and I did my first fire, absolutely terrified. However, the test fires went well and I couldn't wait to paint enough pieces to fill the kiln! I kept notes of how the firing went, so that I could check how my colours had fired at different temperatures.

I must have chattered away at my sewing classes (chattering is another Gemini trait), telling everyone about my china painting. At that time there was no-one in the Wakefield area china painting, so people were curious and wanted to know if I would show them how paint on china. My own teacher encouraged me to start a small group at home.

I hesitate to call it teaching. My friends arrived one Monday morning, I showed them how I had started and that was it, they wanted to know more. Managing to keep one step ahead of my 'students' meant I had to work hard and not just at china painting, I was still a full-time housewife and mother.

Monday mornings commenced with; breakfast for everyone, take the dog for a short walk, take daughter to school, come home, clean out stable of daughter's pony, feed pony etc., dash inside, wash thoroughly, change clothes and be ready at 9.30am to work with my 'students'. We always had tea and coffee and cookies. My group would leave at approx. 12.30pm through the front door and I would rush out and walk the dog again, grab my china painting gear and rush off to Harrogate for the next 'lesson'. Phew! Rush home to make tea, walk dog etc. etc. etc.

China painting in the UK had always been in a very traditional style, painting with fat oil and turpentine but we were very lucky that Flo had been introduced to copaiba balsam. Copaiba balsam stayed workable for much longer, this allowed us to blend our colours more freely, but we could only have a tiny bottle each, as copaiba was not easily available. Square shaders were also very rare items - it feels as if I am writing about Stonehenge! It was 1980 and my one and only square shader was worn to a round shader before I could purchase another one. Now, of course, brushes are more readily available and my medium is an open medium, aptly named "Gemini".

By this time I had been told about the American china painting magazines and organisations also a Convention in Detroit, USA in July 1980. Peter said he wasn't going to go and watch china painting for a week, but, I had never been anywhere on my own, dare I go? There were so many questions I had to ask someone about my new hobby, so I made up my mind to go! I was really pleased when Peter changed his mind and decided to go with me.

Well, it was fantastic. Thousands of people all with the same interest. So much to see and do, I could not decide what to do first, which demonstration to see, what to buy? Many famous china painters demonstrating, ones who I had only read about in the books and magazines. I had been corresponding with Ruth Little for some time, asking her questions about things I did not understand in my china painting. Ruth and her husband and daughter were so good to Peter and I, they really looked after us and introduced us to many people who I still visit and write to today. During the convention people kept asking what was going on in UK, were there any seminars there? All the way home after the convention I kept thinking about seminars.

We lived in quite a large old house that we had purchased in a mad moment, and so far we had only renovated half of it. "Why couldn't we fix up the rest of the house and run seminars at home?" I asked Peter. You know what men are like, they just love to ignore imaginative remarks. Meanwhile I had been asked to teach at the local nightschool and do several demonstrations locally, so I found I was getting more and more involved in this new hobby.

As word got around that there would be seminars at "Westfield House" after June the following year, hundreds of enquiries from around the world rolled in and my family wanted to know what I was going to do now. "Panic!" I suggested if we did a bit more redecorating we would easily handle everything. Little did I know that life would never be quite the same again.

China painters overseas have always been fascinated by the traditional techniques of our famous china painting companies, so we asked artists who had trained at places such as Wedgwood, Minton, Spode and Worcester if they would be willing to give up their holiday time to come and tutor.

Our first international seminar attracted china painters from around the world, Norway, New Zealand, Denmark, Australia and of course, America. It was like a marvellous house party, everyone thoroughly enjoyed themselves, they learnt a great deal about china painting from the tutors and from sharing their own experiences with their fellow students. We did all the catering ourselves, Peter took time off from his business to do the cooking, luckily it was school holidays so the children helped out with all the chores, peeling mountains of potatoes, washing tons of lettuce for salads, waiting on tables, making beds and all that good stuff. Our 'guests' said it was really wonderful to stay in a home with a family instead of a hotel, and, of course, it was absolute bliss for our 'guests'. A china painters dream, to paint all day whilst someone provided meals at regular intervals and tea and biscuits at just the right moment.

On the 'free' days inbetween seminars we organised day trips to places of interest. Stoke-on-Trent is a must for china painters, also York is very close at hand and packed with things to see. Seminars at "Westfield House" have continued from that first year with many china painters returning again and again to spend their 'holidays' in Wakefield and enjoy the 'magic' of china painting.

Over the years, I collected so many hints, recipes and line drawings from our tutors and guests I decided to start a newsletter. I typed up A4 sheets, then took them to the photo copy shop, these sheets were given away to interested china painters. The demand for the 'Westfield House News' grew, and so did the cost of the photo copies. The time came to give up, or do something more positive with the 'News". Our first colour magazine went out in June 1984. The first year we only produced three magazines . It seemed so popular, we decided to do four the following year, our subscribers said it was not enough we then moved to six issues per year. Now our magazine, "The British Porcelain Artist" is well established and is sent around the world to all interested subscribers.

The magazine, like the seminars, is very much a family effort. My son, Glen, helps to put the magazine together, his wife, Janice, keeps the membership files up to date in her spare time. My daughter, Jan, helps when the filing gets beyond belief and everyone has to assist when it comes to sticking labels on envelopes and packing magazines. Peter and I are lucky enough to have three grandchildren. Glen and Janice have two boys, Adam and Sam, and Jan and Chris have a daughter, Gemma. It's nice to have such a fantastic family who cope so well with everything.

China painting has made us many friends around the world and in the UK. It is wonderful to visit other countries and share your knowledge and friendship with others. Being asked to demonstrate at different china painting events makes you work hard to achieve new goals in your own work, you gain so much from the enthusiasm of other china painters. "More magic" to keep you learning and painting in your own china painting world.

Over the years I have been invited to many places around the world. I really enjoy my annual visit to Scotland to demonstrate there, the Scottish hospitality is really something. Peter and I have visited our many friends in Norway and I have demonstrated at one of their china painting shows . Our visit to Australia gave us the chance to see our relatives before taking part in a show in Brisbane. I have been invited to demonstrate in the USA many times, and we enjoy seeing our friends from the china painting world when we visit the conventions in various States in the USA. Peter usually takes 'time out' to play a little golf in the sun on our trips. Who would think that a hobby would bring invitations to teach and demonstrate from so many countries, France, Spain, Portugal, Dubai, Germany, Italy, Brazil, Uruquay, Ecuador and Switzerland. I really need an extra day in every week!

Since taking up china painting - even when I have not had much time - I have always tried to improve my own painting and learn as much as possible about everything to do with this wonderful art form. Learning is a never ending process. There is always a new challenge to meet and never enough time to do all the things you want to do. Through the years I hope I have learnt a great many things. I know I have met many wonderful people, encouraged a great number of others to take up china painting, and given some china painters the confidence to go out and teach others the great pleasure that can come from enjoying a very relaxing and creative hobby. Some people just wish to have pleasant company once a week with something 'unique' at the end of their class. Others find it a marvellous chance to have a hobby which will provide them with hand painted pieces to sell at craft fairs etc., wedding plates, christening plates and special occasion pieces are always in demand.

There are those who get all 'fired' up to spread the word and teach others this fascinating art. All find a satisfaction in what they do and each has something to share with the other.

I have now reached the 'still age'. People I see now and then 'non china painters of course', ask me "Celia are you 'still' china painting?" "Just a bit" I reply.

I do hope you will enjoy china painting as much as I do !
CELIA.

**Design for Baby
Plate**

SO YOU WANT TO BE A CHINA PAINTER

Discovering a new hobby is very exciting, along with the initial excitement comes the thirst for knowledge and the desire to purchase the essential equipment needed to pursue your new hobby. " How do I learn more about china painting?" is one of the first questions asked.

You may have seen some hand painted china on display somewhere and admired the artist's work. A few enquiries may lead you to a class at your local night school where you will find others who are also learning more about this interesting hobby.

"What supplies do I need to start china painting"?

Personally I feel you should begin with the very basic items, then wait until you get to class and be advised by your teacher. Your teacher will recommend certain basic colours, the brushes and medium to use for your new hobby, your teacher will also show you their china painting technique. As you progress you will try other mediums (oils), brushes and colours and will eventually decide which items from your collection you prefer to use yourself, to develop your own style.

Every china painter is looking for a 'magic' brush that will load itself with paint, dance across the plate and produce a wonderful finished masterpiece all by itself. If you have found such a marvellous item - do let me know - I want one too!

A selection of china painting equipment and a palette of colours that have been mixed.

List of requirements:

Brushes: The traditional china painting brush is made of squirrel hair and comes in a quill with a plain wooden handle. Also there are various lines of brushes in metal ferrules with painted coloured handles. You will probably start out with the brushes your teacher recommends, and along the way you will try different brushes. Like most things, brushes are very personal and you will find favourite brushes which you use all the time.

If starting the naturalistic technique - a middle sized square shader No 8, number 4 square shader and a scroller brush or fine line brush would be enough to begin with.

Medium: The medium is the oil which you use to paint with and everyone prefers different mediums. Your teacher may use one oil to mix paints with - mixing medium - and another oil to paint with - painting medium. Again this is a personal choice and you will no doubt experiment with different mediums until you decide which one you like best. Gemini is the name of the medium I use, I mix my paints with it and paint with it. Once you have decided on your favourite 'magic' medium then you can concentrate on learning to paint. All mediums are burnt away during the firing process leaving just the paint on the china.

Palette: A covered palette to keep your mixed colours in: This could be a plastic food box with an airtight lid and a tile inside for your palette. You could use an ordinary household wall tile for your palette. A second tile can be kept just for mixing your paints on.

Other useful things:
Palette Knife
Stabilo Pencil: For sketching on the china.
Tracing paper and a sheet of light grey graphite paper.
Flat dish for medium and a small screw top jar for your turps. (Artists turps or a good brush cleaner is used to clean your brushes).
Kitchen roll or better still, pieces of cotton cloth in handy squares.
Piece of silk - for wiping out highlights.
Pen for penwork - a good nib is a priority, the nib should not spread when you apply pressure.
Wooden cocktail sticks - for wiping out or of course you can purchase wipe out tools.
Sandpaper: This must be extremely fine sandpaper - to gently rub down your china after firing.
Small medium dropper to use when adding drops of your medium when mixing your colours.

Colours: Colour to begin with is very confusing - so many colours - so many different names. Try to establish a few good colours as your limited palette.

Light yellow, yellow brown, a warm brown, malachite - this is a turquoise blue, royal blue, a good pink, a light green, a medium bright green, dark green or black green, black. Maroon - or a good American Beauty and pink pompadour. These colours should start you off and you will add to them as you go along.

Reds: Your teacher will give you lots of advice about colours. China painters always have difficulty with reds - reds do not usually mix with yellows in china painting. Don't forget the colours have to be fired in a kiln, so the reactions of the metals in the colours and the glaze on the china often has 'exciting' results that you hadn't anticipated.

Test firing: New colours are coming onto the scene all the time and the latest 'yellow for reds' does seem to work quite well when mixed with reds. You will find pink pompadour gives good results. it is a nice easy colour to work with and not gritty. The traditional way of obtaining red is to paint a good yellow orange onto the area you require to be red, e.g. an apple or part of a peach, fire 800°C. Next fire, paint over the yellow orange with a good pink to give you your red, fire 780°C.

However it is useful to make a test firing of all your colours yourself and that way you will have a record for your own reference. All you need is an old plate or tile, paint on a line or square of colour, don't forget to 'name' it - use your fine liner and china paint to write the name at the side of the paint then you will have an excellent reference for future painting, after the tile has been fired.

Mixing the paint: Your paint will usually come as powder in a small glass or plastic bottle. You need your clean mixing tile, palette knife and medium to mix the paint with, kitchen roll to clean up afterwards. Palette to receive the mixed colours.

Start by tipping some of the powder china paint onto the centre of your mixing tile. Add a few drops of medium to this 'pile' of paint and with the palette knife, mix the paint and oil together well. If the paint is at all 'gritty' put pressure on the palette knife when mixing, this will 'grind' the paint between knife and tile, hopefully the paint will become smoother. The paint should have a 'toothpaste' consistency; if it is too oily, add more powder paint, if it is too dry add a drop more oil. When you are satisfied with the mixture, scoop it all together and transfer it to your palette. Always placing the colours on your palette in the same place, this will be a great help to you as a painter. You will always know exactly where that colour is on your palette. Mark out the palette in squares, write the name of the colour on the palette with your stabilo pencil Always clean the mixing tile thoroughly after each colour is mixed.

Condition your brush: It is important to take great care of your brushes, a new brush needs to be conditioned in the medium before it is used. Your new square shader in a quill comes as a fluffy, round, soft haired brush. Dip the hair of the brush into your medium, then press the heel of the brush down onto the tile; wiggle the brush on the tile, pulling the brush towards you, this will make the hairs of the brush fan out on the tile. This then is your square shader. If you use an open medium (one that NEVER dries), after conditioning the brush you can blot off the excess oil; this is done by pressing the bristles onto a clean cloth with your finger. Don't press and pull the hairs or you will break the hairs in the brush. You can work excess medium out of your brush by working the brush on your mixing tile. If you know that the medium dries, you should clean the medium out of your brush as soon as you have finished painting by swishing the brush well in turps. or your chosen brush cleaner. Gently flatten it out to its chisel shape with your fingers and store it in your brush box. Be extremely careful not to press the hairs up to the edge of a box and 'bend' them, or trap them, as it is so difficult to 'revive' them after this sort of treatment. I always leave mine standing, bristle end up in an old tankard and cover them loosely with a plastic bag if I am not painting for some time. I know some people do not recommend this but I find it is convenient for me.

Choosing your china: Ordinary white ceramic tiles are always cheap and readily available, white porcelain can be bought in many large stores. Bone china is available sometimes on market stalls, but to start with it would be better to be guided by your teacher or one of the suppliers of white china.

Starting to paint: You will find bone china is much whiter than porcelain. Bone china usually has a lovely glaze when painted and fired, porcelain is sometimes a little more 'matt' looking.

By this time you will be really excited and raring to go. You can sketch your design onto the china by using a stabilo pencil, or perhaps you prefer to trace a design onto tracing paper. Next, place the tracing paper onto the china, make sure you like the position of the design, use sellotape to secure the design to the china down one side of the tracing. Place your sheet of graphite (carbon paper) underneath the tracing paper and go around the tracing with a stylus or an empty biro. Remove the tracing paper and graphite paper. A complicated outline can be 'held' a little more permanently by going over the main graphite outline with an 8046 stabilo pencil. You will find this pencil line does not move when you start painting. Your teacher may recommend a fine, black felt pen that can be used to go over your lines. The traditional method for the outline is to use a chinese ink stick. Dip the end of the ink stick into water, rub the ink stick on a tile or dish, you will have 'ink'. Use a fine brush to apply the ink over your graphite lines. When the ink is dry you can paint over the design with your china paint, the lines will fire away in the kiln..

If you are following a study you will have your procedure sheet in front of you, or perhaps you are following your teacher step by step. To load your brush with paint, dip the brush into your medium, work the brush on your tile by wiggling it towards you and blot out excess oil onto a clean cloth or work the excess oil off on your tile. Now work the brush into your pile of colour, test it on your tile to see how much colour you have, then start work on your plate. Try not to get the work too oily as too much oil will collect lint and dust from the atmosphere. This dust fires away but sometimes there is a mark in the paint where the dust has been.

Clean the brush well between each new colour used, re-oil the brush and go into the next colour and so on.

As you progress it is best to work from the lightest colour up to the darkest, this way you do not need to clean your brush as often.

Don't overwork the piece and don't forget if you are not satisfied with the result you can clean off the plate and start again. Until your plate is 'fired' in the kiln nothing is permanent.

Happy painting! Celia.

13

PANSIES

Pansies are delightful flowers to have in the garden. Every day through the spring and summer their smiling faces bring cheer to those who take the time to look at them. Now of course there are winter varieties which add colour to even the gloomiest days.

Each year I promise myself that I will sketch and paint nothing else but pansies all summer long, 'day dreams'. It is usually winter time before I manage to get down to painting, so I often use old calendars, photographs or antique cards as references and also any sketches I have made during the year. I paint flower studies, from life, using water colours, this is also a wonderful way of getting to know the flower you are studying.

I sketched the pansies onto the tile with a chinagraph pencil, then I took a tracing of the finished design in case I needed it again. Before I start painting, I try to make sure I have the colours I will need mixed ready to use.

Colours used: For this study I used perfect pink, sevres blue, pink purple, royal purple, blackberry purple, albert yellow, mixing yellow, capacine red, violet of iron, chartreuse, antique green, black green, and grey.

Commencing with the pansy at the top of the design, take a small square shader and apply a thin wash of perfect pink to the petals. You may find a medium square shader more useful for the larger petals. By starting at the back of the flower you can make sure of the petal shapes by wiping out any light shapes as you move forward, or if the petal edges are darker, you can add some pink purple, mix the two colours together in the brush, then apply the colour to the china. Don't forget when your piece of china is fired your pencil lines will have disappeared and you will need to be able to 'find' your design.

Leave the buds until last, you need to be able to work freely without worrying about smudging detailed work.

Chartreuse and cool green were used on the first fire for the leaves and the sepals and stems.

Perfect pink, pink purple, sevres blue and albert yellow were used for the pansies on either side of the central pansy. Carefully place your colours, clean excess colour from your brush and then gently blend where the colours meet. Do not be tempted to paint the faces of the pansies on this fire - just a wash of colours to use as a base on the next fire. Clean any unwanted colour from the central pansy. Capacine red was used for the orangey area and mixing yellow for the yellow area. Be very careful to place the colours, blend slightly and leave them alone. Paint the rest of the leaves, then use pink purple and royal purple for the darkest pansy The buds can now be painted lightly. Fire cone 017 or 780°C.

Second fire: If you feel your design isn't quite right, you can check to see if you have left anything out by placing your tracing of the design over your plate. Sketch or trace on any missing petals or leaves.

The second fire in this case means adding darker colours to the design, pink purple and blackberry purple were used on the flower at the top of the design, antique green and black green were the colours used to darken the leaves. Don't forget to leave some of the light colours used on the first fire to shine through. Pink purple, sevres blue, blackberry purple and royal purple were used on the flowers on each side of the central flower. Once again, clean any unwanted colour from the central flower. Carefully darken the capacine and the mixing yellow if you feel it is necessary. Use grey to shade the areas on the mixing yellow. Violet of iron will give you the colour for the 'whiskers' on this flower; paint them on with a medium pointed brush. Blackberry purple, royal purple and the pink purple will mix together in your brush and give you a dark rich colour for the bottom flowers. The same mix can be used for the 'whiskers' on the other pansies. Strengthen the colours on the buds. fire cone 017 or 780°C.

Third fire: Use a large background brush or your largest square shader for the washes of background colours. Do not make the background too dark or you will 'take away' from your flowers. Make sure you do not introduce different colours at this stage, use colours from your design. Fire 018 cone. or 770°C.

Pansies

Colour on page 19

PENWORK

Q. What is meant when china painters talk about penwork and when would I use it?

A. Often beginners find china painting much easier if they have a design which can be penned on first and then painted with colours.

Firstly trace or sketch your design onto your piece of china. Then, using your palette knife, mix your ordinary china paint powder with pen oil on a mixing tile to an ink consistency. Use an old fashioned dip pen or a mapping pen with a steel nib, turn the pen upside down and scoop up some of the 'ink' with the pen. For the ink to flow freely from the nib you will find that you need to hold the pen more upright and to give the ink time to run off the pen nib.

If you do not have any pen oil you could mix the china paint powder with some icing sugar and then add a few drops of water until you achieve the correct ink consistency. Any mistakes you make can be corrected (when the pen work is dry) by scratching off unwanted lines with a cocktail stick. Usually it is easier to fire at this stage but if you wish to get on with your painting (when the penwork is really dry) you may find you can paint over the pen work with your colours.

Shopping Day
Colour on page 18.

Celia
Shute.

**Shopping
Day**

**April
Showers**

Pansies

THE SMILING COTTAGE

Colours used: Malachite (or baby blue), mixing yellow, pink, moss green, shading violet, violet of iron, celadon green, light red, grey, yellow orange, rich brown.

First fire: Sketch or trace the design onto your china. There is no need to sketch every flower. If you place the cottages and the two silver birch trees correctly you will be able to ad-lib slightly with the rest of the picture. With landscapes it is usually advisable to start at the 'back' of the picture and work forward.

First I painted the sky with malachite, mixing yellow and pink, using a medium sized square shader. Carefully place the colours where you want them, then blend carefully. Do not 'mix' them together or your sky will not have the 'pretty' colours we are aiming for.

Next work on the area of trees behind the silver birches. Use a soft pointed brush to stipple on your colours (the 'O' portrait brush does a good job). Try not make the area too solid or too stippled. The colours used in this area were; moss green, shading violet, violet of iron and celadon green for the green bank area. Wipe out the colour from the tree trunks. Leave the twiggy branches at this time. Now, carefully colour your cottage, light red for the chimneys. Shading violet and moss green for the roof and grey to indicate the windows and door. Use moss green and yellow orange for the distant and central trees. With grey and shading violet take a fine liner and draw in the shapes of the distant houses.

If you are exhausted by now, just give the foreground a light wash of colours, using a touch of malachite for the water area. More work and details can be added on a second fire. Don't forget to wipe out your figure standing on the bank. Fire 780°C.

Second fire: You may need to strengthen your sky colours a little - not too much. Next your trees behind the silver birches and any details on your house, red roofs for the distant houses. Darken the river bank in front of the figure with rich brown. Carefully paint a little colour onto the figure. If you overpaint her she will not look right in the landscape. Wipe any unwanted colour off the silver birches. Grey and rich brown can be used to shade the silver birches, use grey on a fine liner for the twiggy branches. Indicate a few leaves (with your pointed brush) on the branches.

Mix moss green and brown in your brush for the dark areas in the water. Paint in and wipe out the reeds and grasses along the river bank and also the flowers. Fire 770°C. Colour on page 22.

April Showers

Colour on page 18

Smiling Cottage

Fantasy Peacock

Tanya and Blossom

FANTASY PEACOCK

Perhaps like me you sometimes see colours and designs that you think would look well on certain pieces of china that you have in your 'store' cupboard. You can't wait to get time to try them out. This particular design I started because I thought it would be a nice easy project for my class. Occasionally I do have slight fantasies like that. Of course, once I had started it I realised it was going to be a long project . By the time I had finished it classes were through for the year!

Colours used: A good strong blue (sevres blue or banding blue), mixing yellow, perfect pink, ochre, malachite, moss green, midnight blue.

This design was painted on an oval platter with a rim. Carefully sketch or trace the main design on to your plate, do not bother with the outside rim at this stage. Test fire your blues and use one that holds well, banding blue, sevres blue or something similar. This blue will be used for all the line work on the first fire, which was done with a pen. When the centre part is complete you can trace on the 'eyes' around the outside rim. If you mark the centre ones, top and bottom and the sides, then you can space the remaining ones inbetween. Use your own judgment to balance them around the rim, use penwork for this area. Fire 780°C. Cone 017.

Second fire: You can paint resist over the 'eye' areas on the main design first, or wash your colours over the feathered area and then 'clean' up the paint from the unwanted areas.

Wash a little yellow, a good pink and blue over the fan of feathers, blend well - not too much. Clean excess paint from the 'eye' areas and the peacock. Carefully paint the light yellow in the 'eyes', don't forget the centre blue has to be kept clean. The feather area behind the birds body and feet are also yellow. His body needs a wash of blue paint.

Moss green for the foreground and the area behind the fan, carefully clean the rim. Repeat the washes of colour lightly around the rim (blue, pink and yellow). Clean out the 'eye' areas. Paint in the light yellow colour. Check carefully you have 'cleaned out' everywhere you need to. Fire 770°C. Cone 017.

Third fire: You may need to strengthen the colours on the fan of feathers, clean off 'eye' areas once more. Strengthen colours on bird. Paint the blues in the eye areas, using malachite or baby blue for the light blue and your banding blue and midnight blue for the dark. Repeat procedure for the rim. Fire 770°C . Cone 017.

Fourth fire: Bright gold was used stippled on with a sponge on the bottom area of the feathers and gold bands were applied. Fire gold to 740°C. Cone 019. Colour on page 22

Fantasy Peacock.
Colour on page 22

Celia Shute.

25

Benjie

Firm Friends

**Lustre Designs
by
Glen Shute**

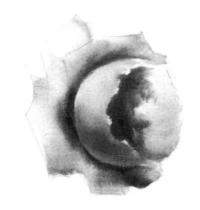

1

2

3

4

HOW TO PAINT ROSES

The allure and romance of the rose has fascinated man throughout the ages. For centuries it has inspired not only artists and poets but mankind as a whole. It seems that no one can resist the Queen of Flowers. China painters are just as bewitched as everyone else and we all long to paint the perfect rose. Here's hoping that these simple instructions will help in some way with your rose painting

1. Visualise a fluffy rose. With a stabilo pencil lightly sketch your rose on to your china. Only the base essentials, too many petals at this point will confuse you later. A medium square shader will be the best brush and an open medium, pink pompadour will be the easiest colour to use. Turn the rose on its side, so to speak and paint the heart of the rose, getting a depth of paint in the throat of the rose.

2. Whilst painting you will need to keep turning the china to make sure you are pulling your brush strokes towards yourself. Turn the rose upside down, paint the bowl of the rose shading the shadow side with a little more colour.

3. Now the rose is on its side again, paint in the shadow under the bowl. Each time we turn the rose we are painting towards ourselves. Then, put a flat wash of colour across the rest of the petals.

4. Paint a soft tint of your background colours around the rose (it is right side up now). Start wiping out your petals, condition your brush in your medium , press out all the excess oil from your brush onto a cloth (press the brush between your finger and the cloth) your square shader should now have a chisel edge to it.

Use the square edge of the brush to cut across where you want your petal to be, pull the paint down towards yourself for the turned over part of the petal, or turn the rose upside down and push the paint away from the straight edge you have cut. I'm afraid it is only practice and experience which will tell you where to make the cuts for the petals.

Look at the overall shape of your rose, make less petal cuts rather than more, step ladders are easy to create. As your confidence grows so will your roses.

ANIMALS

My very first request for an animal portrait was for a painting of a Cavy. As I had no idea what a Cavy was the first thing I had to do was make a trip to the library and find out what sort of animal I had been asked to paint.

I was sent a line drawing showing its markings. These were very important as the Cavy had won all sorts of prizes at shows etc. A black and white picture found in a library book was my only other source. Luckily the colour of the Cavy was black and white so I managed to produce a 'portrait' of the animal which pleased its owner tremendously.

Dogs are the usual requests received for birthday presents and Xmas presents. A very unique personal gift for the recipient.

You need a good photograph of your subject. Sometimes you will have to work from a number of photographs. One photo for the way you want the pet to look on the plate, another one or two photos for details. When you have your subject sketched or traced onto the plate, you will need to paint the eyes first and try to capture the "expression". When you start on the animals face, place the lightest colours, then the darkest darks to help give 'likeness' and shape. Use the same procedure for the body, try not to overwork the first fire.

If you are painting tabby cats, leopards, tigers, or animals with black markings, you can place the 'black' markings first, then other colours on the next fire.

To get the feeling of fur use a pointed shader, the 0 portrait brush or the larger animal brush are useful, press down on the dry brush until the hairs seperate, then load with paint. You will find this 'split' brush does a good job of hair painting. When you are satisfied with your painting fire.

Second Fire:

Any washes of colours on the animals should be done now before you start refining the details. Your pointed shader and a fine liner will help your work on long haired subjects. Smooth haired animals such as horses are mainly worked with square shaders and smooth washes, except for the horses manes and tails of course.

Third Fire:

Paint the background first, then add any details to the animal.

**Capacine
Roses and
Penwork**

**Mice and
Roses
Wedding
Design**

Roses in a Glass Vase

CAPACINE ROSES AND PENWORK

Colours used: Capacine red, sevres green, moss green, violet of iron.

This is a simple but pleasing design inspired by a demonstration of Wanda Claphams. Wanda always makes things look so easy. When I got home I decided I must try the technique out for myself, I should say, Wanda did not use capacine red and she did add more background than I have used.

First fire: After sketching the roses on the plate, using a medium sized square shader I painted the roses using capacine red; a lovely colour, nice and smooth to work with and if fired at a low temperature it fires well. After placing the two full roses I used sevres green and some moss green to lay a light wash of background colour around the roses. The next part to be painted was the 'hanging down' rose, then a light wash of the greens over the leaves. Fire 740°C. Cone 019.

Second fire: For the border around the outside edge I used the sevres green. Again this is a good smooth colour and will brush on very evenly. Try to make the shape of the border balance your design, wipe back the curves ready for the penwork with a piece of silk over your finger. Use a dry brush (a pointed sable) to dry brush scrolls around the inside edge of the 'scroll' design. Fire 740°C.

Third fire: Deepen roses, background and leaves where necessary.

Make a mixing of your moss green and pen oil and pen your scrolls around your design. No need for a 'set' pattern, make the scrolls fit your design. Fire 740°C.

Fourth fire: A gold rim around the edge of the plate will finish off your piece of china.
Fire 720 °C.
You can use any of your favourite colours to do this design - hope you enjoy it as much as I did.
Colour on page 30.

Capacine Roses and Penwork.

**Raised Paste,
Gold and Enamel
Work by
Graham Davies**

**Portrait
with Ground
Border**

**Monochrome
Portrait**

ROSES IN A GLASS VASE

Colours used: Red grape, moss green, cool green, ashes of roses, violet of iron, black green.

Trying to think of something different to paint I decided to work on a design of roses in a glass vase, the vase was kept simple and not too large. I think all in all it is quite a balanced design.

First fire: Trace or sketch your design onto the china . As usual I painted the roses first using the colour red grape. Then a wash of colour on the leaves, moss green and cool green; not too much colour on the first fire. The fern and buds were painted on the second fire. Ashes of roses next to indicate the sides of the glass vase. Make sure you keep plenty of light in the 'glass'. Violet of iron was used to create the shadow under the vase. Fire 780°C. 017 cone.

Second fire: Sketch in the ferns and buds.

Now deepen the roses if necessary. Using your greens, darken your leaves, you will find black green useful in the shadow areas and violet of iron to indicate a few veins on the leaves and stems.

The buds are painted using a pointed brush. Taking a small square shader, lightly paint in the ferns.

Try not to over work the area inside the glass vase. Use your greens and violet of iron. Don't forget, things are distorted through glass. Fire 770°C.

There didn't seem to be any need for a background on this plaque and it has been much admired at demonstrations. Colour on page 31.

Celia
Shute.

Roses In A Glass Vase

Fruit Still Life with Plums and Pears

Apples and Grapes

FRUIT STILL LIFE WITH PLUMS AND PEARS

Relaxing, restful and pleasing to look at is how this study feels now I look at it. Originally I painted it for a seminar and since then it has occasionally come out of its box to go on display but apart from that it is in my store cupboard.

Colours used:

Chartreuse, moss green, celadon green, brown-green, dark green, sevres blue, royal violet, turquoise, ashes of roses, yellow brown, light yellow, medium brown, violet of iron, black, American beauty.

Carefully sketch or trace the design onto your china. Make sure you have all the colours needed already mixed on your palette. You do not need the exact colours named, look at your design and then at the colours on your palette, I am sure you will have something similar to use in the painting.

As I am right handed I usually start on the left hand side of this sort of design and work across the plate from back to front.

With a medium sized square shader paint the leaves using chartreuse and moss green, only a light wash on this fire. Clean your brush ready to paint the plum. The plum needs a wash of sevres blue in the light area. Royal violet in the darker area. Wipe any unwanted paint from the earthen pot and, using a clean brush, paint yellow brown in the light area and a good middle brown in the darker area. You need to indicate the inside of the pot and the rim on this fire.

Each time you clean your brush condition it well in your medium and then load with paint.

Use your greens for the leaves, chartreuse, moss, celadon and perhaps some brown green. A fine brush can be used for stalks and stems. The plums are painted next using the sevres blue and royal violet. Light yellow on the light part of the pears, yellow orange and the medium brown on the darker part. The same colours are used to paint the almond and nuts. Shadows can be painted with brown on this fire. Fire 780°C.

Second Fire:

Using ashes of roses and a large background brush, paint the background above the design. As you come across the plate add some turquoise or malachite to the ashes of roses to 'grey' the colour even more. To get the background smooth you can pull the colour over your design and then wipe off any unwanted colour from your design.

Darken the leaves and stems using brown green and dark green. Royal violet and American beauty to darken the plums. Middle brown and violet of iron to darken the 'pot' and the left hand side has a wash of royal violet.

For the pears use your brown and violet of iron once again and a little black on the base of the front pear. Continue with the background in front of the design, darken the shadows with violet of iron and strengthen the colours on the nuts. Fire 770°C.

Third Fire:

Strengthen any colours where needed. Fire 770°C. This design is a good lesson to help you paint fruit and also to try and achieve 'round' objects. Remember the 'light' areas are very important when achieving the roundness of the clay pot and the fruit. Colour on page 38.

Autumn Days

Leopard
Inspired by the work of
Guy Comenech.

White Iris Design

IRIS

Having admired Kay Godshalk's magnificent Iris tiles so many times, I eventually decided to 'have a go' at painting iris's myself. It's not an easy task to capture the delicate frills and flounces of this stately flower.

The design was painted on an 8 x 10 inch bone china tile or plaque, and, of course, the first stage is to sketch or trace your design onto the china.

Colours used: Light grey, dark grey, ashes of roses, yellow for reds, hair brown, seaweed green, dark green, celadon green, apple green.

First fire: Using a light grey, dark grey and ashes of roses, paint in the shadow areas of the centres of the flowers. Start with the flower on the left hand side, as it is 'behind' the main flower. You will find that there is a lot of 'painting in' and 'wiping out' to be done on this piece. Make sure you clean out the highlights thoroughly.

In the area where the standard petal joins the 'stem' the colour used was hair brown. Don't forget, you are only trying to establish your design so do not try to achieve the 'finished' picture. A wash of yellow for reds or albert yellow will indicate the calyx. To 'create' the outside edge of your petals you will have to work on your background area. Celadon green in the light areas, seaweed green and dark green in the dark parts. Using a medium sized square shader, carefully paint around the edges of these large outside petals, overlapping your outline and blending the edges of your paint. Then, wipe out the edges of your petals, trying to capture the feeling of the iris frills. Using your greens, paint a light wash of colour over the background and leaves. Again you are not trying to finish the design in one fire. Wipe out the bud and flower stems. Shade as necessary, using hair brown on the 'sheath like' area of the bud. Check the highlights. Fire 780°C.

Second fire: Using a large background brush wash your background colours in. You may need more washes of colour over the leaves but do not touch the flowers. Clean out the highlights. Fire 770°C.

Third fire: Decide what colours are needed on your iris and wash the colours over the flowers with a medium sized square shader. Then wipe back the lights and strengthen any areas where extra depth is needed. You will probably find this easier to do with a smaller brush or the corner of your medium square shader. Fire 770°C. This is not an easy design, but when finished it gives a great sense of achievement. Colour on page 43.

Colour on page 43.　　　　　**White Iris**

Merry Christmas

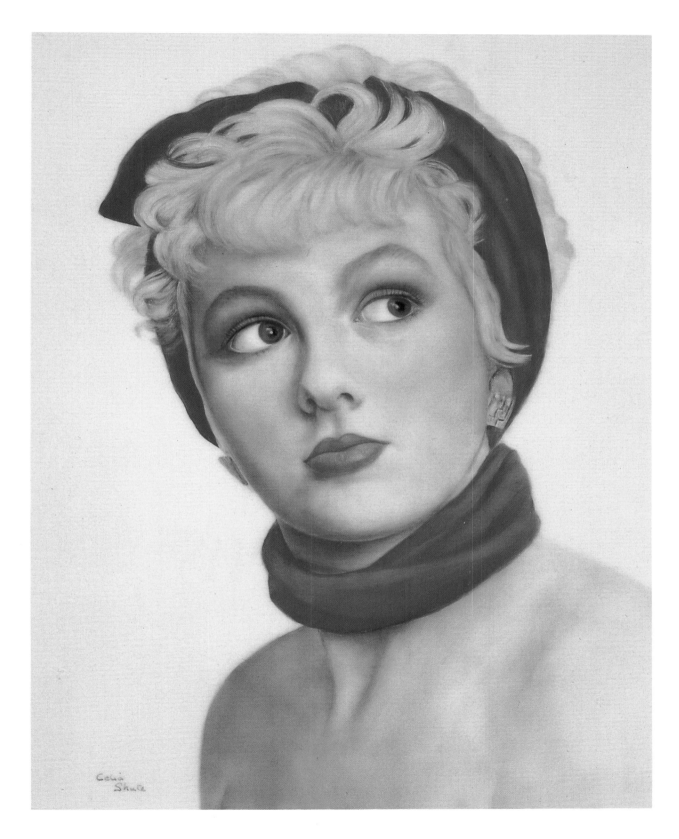

Portrait "Lady in Red"

Christmas Design

CHRISTMAS DESIGN

Every year I think to myself I must paint a Christmas plate but I never seem to get around to painting one. Well, this year I managed to complete a Christmas design with lots of time to spare.

The cheerful Father Christmas came from an old Victorian scrapbook. I added the holly leaves and berries and ,with my grandchildren in mind, I couldn't resist adding some small helpers. I painted the Father Christmas first using some colours from my portrait palette, light red and violet of iron for the face, being careful to keep the highlights. Next, using a good red - portrait light red - I painted his 'hood'. A little light grey on the beard and I wiped out the outer edges of his whiskers.

Using chartreuse and moss green for the holly leaves I worked around the plate, going back to paint the berries and little folk. Fire 750°C.

Second Fire:

The lettering was traced on before I started any painting and I carefully painted the "Merry Christmas" using violet of iron and a fine brush. After that you could fire again or strengthen your colours on Father Christmas and then the holly leaves. You will need dark green and antique green for the leaves. Fire again 750°C.

Colours used:

Light portrait red, violet of iron, light grey, chartreuse, moss green, dark green, antique green. Colour on page 46.

MY FIRST PORTRAIT

If you have never painted a portrait, do try painting a portrait in monochrome. By only using one colour you can concentrate on shapes, light and dark and getting a likeness, no need to worry about which colour goes where. For your first portrait choose something that appeals to you. Pretty girls are usually favourite, wrinkles are not so appealing but they are quite a challenge and lots of fun. You can get away with extra wrinkles if you make a mistake.

My First Portrait 1980. (Colour on page 35).

I didn't know how to start a portrait, what colours or medium to use and where to use which colour, it all seemed very complicated. So I hesitated before I started my first portrait, even though I had purchased special colours and read books about painting portraits it seemed a difficult subject.

Then I watched Lawrence Woodhouse demonstrate portraits using the traditional china painting colours of the Potteries. I couldn't wait to paint a portrait.

The picture I chose to paint was from a print I had bought whilst visiting the National Portrait Gallery in London. It was a picture of Ellen Terry the actress called 'Choosing', by George Frederick Watts. Ellen Terry was married to G.F. Watts in 1864 and they separated in 1865. But I feel they must have been very much in love when he painted the picture.

In the original picture Ellen Terry is shown choosing between camellias and a small bunch of violets in her left hand. I never got around to painting the left hand or the violets. Using a very strong yellow orange colour, Gemini open medium and painting on a ten inch bone china plate, I started painting my version of the portrait early one morning after I had taken the children to school. Before I realised it, I had become entirely engrossed in my painting and did not notice how quickly the time went by. It was soon time to collect the children from school. After dinner I continued and it was early in the morning before I decided that I could not do any more to my piece before it was fired.

I had painted in the dark areas of the picture and wiped out the light areas, trying hard to get the feeling of roundness on the cheek, and make the hair feel like hair. The first fire was 780°C. When the plate came from the kiln I was really pleased with the results. Having no idea what the next step of the process was or how much pink colour to apply on top of the yellow orange, I decided to make this first portrait a monochrome. So I used brown and violet of iron for the next fire, taking care to keep the lights and model the hair, pearls and the clothing details.

Having spent so many hours working on this piece I was terrified it would break in the firing. I paced the floor until I dared open the kiln. Luckily it fired well at 780°C. once more and I felt really elated that it had turned out so well.

When Margaret Winborn came to visit us at Westfield House her wonderful portraits and miniatures painted on porcelain, using subtle colours really made me realise how much I wanted to paint portraits again. After watching Margaret work and listening to her talk about her approach to portrait painting

I felt I was able to use my treasured set of portrait colours at last! Margaret told me to keep working and one day 'Eureka' I would think it had all fallen into place. The trouble is the 'Eureka' marker keeps moving on , and some days it seems a long way ahead of me.

The portrait method used by Jane Marcks also uses subtle portrait colours, Jane has also visited Westfield House and it is marvellous to watch such experts at work.
My own portrait painting has been intermittent over the years, working on your own it takes a little longer to get to your goal, but you learn every step of the way. Learning to 'look" is the most important part of any type of painting, this certainly applies to portrait painting. "Reading" the colours - means looking at the picture you have chosen as your study, and learning to decide which colours will achieve the finished piece. You will find this is a very important part of the learning process. You do not need to paint every portrait colour you have on every piece. Each portrait will be different. Of course there are many studies on the market now, with line drawings and full instructions, so these studies are the best place to begin when you are unsure of where to start with your portraits.

Portrait with Blue Grounded Border. (Colour on P.35)

When I bought this lovely bone china plate I really did not have a subject in mind to paint on it. When I found a birthday card with a pretty lady on the front, I could not resist painting it. First I had to think about the border of the plate; this took two coats of dry grounding using a light turquoise colour. Next I painted the portrait using colours from my portrait palette, some of the turquoise colour that I used on the border was applied to the dress and on the background.

When I felt happy with the portrait and had done the final firing on that, the plate was finished off with a burnish gold line around the inner rim and burnish gold around the 'rope' effect on the edge of the plate.

51

THE LADY IN RED

This is my latest portrait and took me quite a long time to finish, but I feel it was worth all the work. Colour on page 47.

First Fire: Be very careful to take an accurate tracing on clear acetate paper for your portraits. Keep the lines as fine as possible. Using the pale grey graphite under the acetate and transfer your line drawing to the porcelain or china. Check the lines on the porcelain, clean away any unwanted graphite with a wooden cocktail stick.

Eyes - transparency and a little rich brown, light application of black in pupil, wipe out highlight.
Lash line and fold of eyelid - dark brown.
Shadow above lid line- warm shadow.
Tear duct - light red.
Eyebrow - hair brown.
Nostrils and shadows - warm shadow.
Mouth - light red.
Skin - highlights - blond flesh. Shadow area reflected light.
Shadows - warm shadow.
Hair - transparency.
Turban and scarf - red 18.
Earrings - light grey.
Fire 750°C. cone 018.

Second Fire: Give the whole of the skin area a wash of light red, use very lightly and wipe out highlights, leaving a little more light red in cheeks. Darken pupils with rich brown, shade the white of the eyes with grey. Dark brown and a little mahogany for the lid line and fold of eyelid and underneath eye.
Eyebrows - a very fine brush and hair brown.
Lips - light red.
Nostrils violet of iron.
Warm shadow and a little dark brown for the shadows on the skin.
Hair - shade the transparency with hair brown.
Darken the red of the turban and scarf if necessary with red 18. Fire 750°C.
Cone 018.

Third Fire: Wash skin tones with light red where necessary.
Darken eyes if needed and paint pupil with black, wipe out highlights.
Paint lashes very carefully with a fine brush using dark brown.
Check your study and decide if you need to darken any more colours.
Lip line and corner of lips use pompadour.
Shadows under fringe, warm shadow.
Fire 750 °C. Cone 018.

Fourth Fire: You may need another fire to darken where necessary.

Colour on page 47.

Lady in Red

TRADITIONAL RAISED PASTE

A great deal of patience, a steady hand, good co-ordination and a very critical eye was necessary to learn the skills of raised paste. Pattern Gilders (mainly men) had a very long thorough training and they learned the secrets of raised paste from their "time on the bench". Of course now there is not very much done in industry in the way of raised paste, and any pieces that are completed in this way are very expensive items at the end of the process.

Raised paste is supplied to the hobbyist in powder form ready to mix. First grind the raised paste powder with pure turpentine and allow to dry. This helps ensure a smooth mixture. When the paste is dry, halve the mixture and blend it with fat oil on your mixing tile. Just add a little at a time until a smooth stiff mixture is obtained - then add a little pure turps, little by little, mixing well with your palette knife each time until the mixture starts to "string". Then add a little bit more turps, breathing into the mixture at the same time. Be careful with the breath or the mixture will become too "sharp". Mix until you can pick up a small ball of the paste on the point of a brush without it leaving a point in the mixture. This mixture should now make a stroke which gradually diminishes in height from the beginning to the end of the stroke. You should now be able to get the three dimensional quality which is the skill of hand raised paste. It doesn't matter if all the strokes are not the same height as this destroys the effect, you want it to look "hand done".

When the work has dried, make a mixture which is sharper than the previous one by breathing into it more and sometimes you may need to add a little fat oil. With this mixture you can add the finest strokes on top of the work you have already done. This is known as "cutting up" and will be seen when the work is gilded and burnished. Fine graduated dots may be added at this time. Take a small spot of raised paste on the tip of the brush - form the first dot, then with the remaining paste in the brush form the subsequent dots which will diminish as the paste is gradually used up from the brush.

Brushes needed: Small squirrel hair or sable tracers (pointers) with at least three quarters of an inch length of hair to give the necessary "spring" are ideal brushes. Numbers O and OO are the usual size. These fine brushes can also be used for the gold to cover the paste. Make sure you condition your brush well by filling it with raised paste so that it forms a good shape before you start to work. This will make it possible to form a longer stroke.

Practice: It is always better to practice first on a tile. The paste you use for practising can be scraped off the tile with your palette knife and re-mixed. As you work you will find the paste has to be frequently mixed on the tile as it "skins over" making the mixture difficult to pick up on the brush. Also, this means that the turps. in the mixture is gradually converted to fat oil so the other half of your original mixture can be used to keep the paste workable. Always work pulling the brush strokes towards yourself.

Weather Conditions: Different weather conditions can alter the consistency of the paste mixture, a damp day will require 'less' breath.

Firing: There is no need for the paste to dry before firing, providing you do not fire the kiln too quickly. The temperature needed to fire raised paste is 720°C. - 1328F - Cone 019.
After firing the paste should look almost the same as it did before - matt.

Covering the raised paste: A high quality gold that is unfluxed must be used for covering the raised paste. Liquid burnish gold is not suitable for this job as it is just absorbed by the paste and fires black.

The alphabet and numbers below were done by Graham Davies especially for Westfield House seminars.

APPLES AND GRAPES

When my students requested a further fruit design to go with the pears and plums I decided to use another one of Catherine Klein's beautiful designs as the study for our lesson.

Colours used:

Background colours. Once again ashes of roses and malachite.
Leaves. Yellow brown, moss green, brown green, dark green.
Dark grapes. Perfect pink, black grape, sevres blue.
Pink grapes. Ruby purple, perfect pink, sevres blue, American beauty.
Apples: Light yellow, yellow brown, seaweed green, perfect pink, black.
Stems. Violet of iron.
Nuts. Yellow orange, medium brown, violet of iron.
Stonework. Seaweed green and grey.

First Fire: Use the lightest colours for washes of colour on the leaves. Grapes always look easy, but don't forget they need to be kept 'round' if they are round grapes, oval if they are oval grapes.

Paint the grapes at the back first, then work forward. Don't try to put on too much paint at once, keep the light areas.

The apples can be painted with the lightest colours, do not try to apply pink on this fire.

For the pink grapes try to find nice 'grit free' colours to work with, this will make the painting of the grapes a little easier. Use a small square shader and perhaps a pointed brush will help you get the colour onto the right area. Check the shapes and light areas before you fire. You can use a pointed sable or a wipe out tool for the highlight. Paint the stems lightly with violet of iron. Paint the almonds using yellow brown and a middle brown. Fire 800°C. cone 016.

Second Fire: You may need to gently use a very fine sandpaper to sand off any roughness on your china. Then use your background brush or a large square shader to apply the colour to the background. Clean any unwanted paint from the design.

Darken your leaves, not too much, use dark green in the darkest area. A wash of pink all over the dark grapes, then darken the dark grapes with black grape. Add any shading you feel necessary to the apples, yellow brown and seaweed green, then apply the pink. You may find a pointed shader does a good job on this part of the design. Place the black at the base of the apple.

Ruby purple and a little sevres blue in places can be washed over all the 'pink' grapes. Clean out highlights and add dark areas with American beauty.

Continue with the background, carefully around the bottom part of the design. Darken the almonds using violet of iron.   Paint the shadows on the stonework. Fire 770°C. cone 017.

Third Fire: Darken design where necessary.
I hope you don't get lost amongst the grapes - it does make a nice 'pair' to the other fruit design!

Apples and Grapes

THE KILN

Access to a kiln is essential to your new hobby of china painting. Your teacher will probably have her own kiln, or use the kiln provided at the local Further Education Centre and do a 'Firing Service' for her students.

If you get really hooked on your hobby you will no doubt look around for a kiln, don't forget you will get years of pleasure from this new hobby so start your letter to Santa now.

Some years ago the only kilns available in the U.K. were specially built for potters, they were very solid, heavy kilns which took a long time to heat up and cool down. Now kilns are made just for china painters, they can be run from ordinary 13 amp sockets in the garage, cellar or utility room.

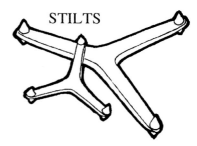

TOP LOADING KILN

What size kiln: You have to decide what sort of things you are going to paint. Are you going to fire other people's china? This will certainly help you decide what size of kiln you need. If you purchase too large a kiln you may feel you have to fill it, if too small you may be frustrated because you haven't enough room in the kiln. There are top loading kilns and front loading kilns. Decisions...decisions....

Front loading kilns allow you to see exactly where you are loading your china, but usually they take up a little more room in the home. The top loading kiln can be moved about more easily, in case you need the space for something else.

Ask if the kiln has an automatic shut off!

Does it have a pyrometer read out?

Follow the manufacturer's instructions for firing and you will find it very easy to use.

Kiln furniture: This refers to the shelves and props that help you 'stack' the china in your kiln. T cranks are good for stacking lots of plates or tiles, they do not take as long to heat up or cool down as shelves. Kiln shelves do not go right across the kiln, this allows the air to circulate in the kiln.

STILTS

Use the props (posts) to support one shelf on top of another, use one at each side of the shelf at the front and one at the centre of the shelf at the back. Three cornered stilts can be used to raise some of your china above the shelf to allow the air to circulate around them.

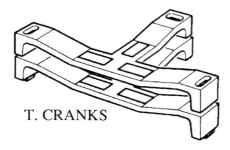

T. CRANKS

Stacking the kiln: Stack the kiln carefully. Don't forget bone china must not touch the sides of the kiln or any other piece of china, its soft glaze will melt and the china will stick to other pieces (if they are touching), during the firing process. Porcelain has a much harder glaze so pieces of porcelain can touch one another and the shelves of the kiln and fire perfectly well.

Bone China: Bone china needs a nice slow firing, this means taking the heat of the kiln up slowly and allowing the kiln to cool right down before taking out the bone china.

Porcelain: Porcelain can be fired more quickly, if required, raising the temperature of the kiln more quickly and taking the porcelain pieces out of the kiln before it is completely cool, but if you are not in a hurry there is no need to tempt fate.

Firing The Kiln: As far as I know kilns made in UK have a safety interlocking arrangement that makes sure the lid of top loading kilns cannot be lifted, or the door of front loading kilns opened when the kiln is switched on. The power is switched off when the lid or door is opened.

Mini Bars: If your kiln is controlled by mini-bars or small cones, these usually fit into a kiln sitter, the kiln sitter requires a new mini-bar or small cone each time the kiln is fired.

These mini-bars have different numbers, 016, 017 and so on, this is relevant to the temperature that they fire at, 016 is approx. 800 deg. cent, 1458 deg F. When the kiln reaches the correct temperature the mini-bar bends and the off switch is automatically triggered to switch off.
Mini-bars work on 'heat work' and you may find the firing temp. may very slightly.

Kilns With Energy Regulator: Once you have switched on the kiln at the socket, the Energy regulator control provides the means of regulating the input of the electricity. The technical details are too complicated for me (this page deals with the very basics). The Energy Regulator control has numbers 1.2.3.4.5. Do follow any instructions that have come with your kiln. Usually the instructions say to set the Energy Regulator to 1 - 2 for one hour with the bungs out.

Set the temperature control to the temperature you require. As the temperature in the kiln rises the mediums you have used will start to burn off and you will notice a slight smell.

After one hour you turn the Energy Regulator to 3 - 4 for one and a half hours, at this stage put in the bungs. When the kiln has reached 500 deg. turn the Energy Regulator to full. If your kiln has an automatic shut off it will turn off at the temp. you have set it to. Be very careful if you have to watch the temperature and turn the kiln off yourself - don't fall asleep!

All makes of kiln vary and as it is some time since I bought my kiln I am not up to date with all the new gadgets that are available. The computer age has reached the kilns and there are some excellent controls available giving much more control of the firing process.

A kiln that is really full will, of course, take a longer time to fire and cool down afterwards.

FRONT LOADING KILN

HINTS ON LUSTRE

1. The hard and fast rule with lustre is that all china brushes and plates etc. must be scrupulously clean.

2. As to the cleaning of china here ideas vary a great deal. One idea is to clean the china first with lustre thinners, do not use turps. as this could react with the lustre.

Others who have used lustre for many years clean their plates with turps. One thing everyone agrees about is never wash the plates or put water near them as this reacts with the lustre and can cause the white spots we hear so much about.

3. Try to avoid dust settling on the lustre as this will fire as whitish blotches, so cover immediately.

4. To keep lustre open longer add a little lavender oil or one of the lustre thinners available today.

5. If you want a dark shade, it is far better to have repeated tintings and firings rather than try to get one thick coat on which will fire to a powder and then rub off.

6. Some lustres are difficult to use and are best avoided until more experience has been gained.

7. To pad smoothly, hold plate almost vertical to avoid as much dust as possible, apply even pressure, continue padding until the lustre sounds tacky.

8. Padding causes a lighter tint than brushing.

9. You cannot use lustres over dusted grounds and only over very delicate tints, even this requires a great deal of experience to gauge the consistency of the lustre and the paint to avoid a matt effect.

10. If you have a design to pen in first, use sugar water to mix your paint and draw in your design with a mapping pen, the sugar water will not affect the lustres.

11. Some people say that lustre needs a strong firing, others a low one. This is where you have to find out for yourself. I know that in Norway some lustres are fired at 800°C, but don't forget that this is on porcelain and with lustres especially made for porcelain. Here in England most people fire at 720 - 750°C.

12. It is advisable to leave the door of the kiln open (if possible) until the lustre dries and the fumes evaporate. But this is only done with large quantities. One or two pieces do not produce enough humidity to affect the result.

13. Smoke in the kiln will affect the brilliancy of the colours.

14. Lustres can be fired with other colours, although colours on other pieces may affect your lustres. Keep your lustre away from the elements and towards the middle of the shelf has been the advice I have been given.

15. Light lustres are more reliable than dark lustres.

16. Above all, lustres are always unpredictable, many things will alter the fired results - varying degrees of heat, different china, firing methods, kilns etc.

17. Shake the lustre before using it. It is also advisable when storing lustre to give the bottles a shake every now and then as this stops the salts from settling. Lustres are best stored in a cool place - the fridge is a good example but make sure to label them well.

Applying Lustre:

If you have never used lustre before please take great care to work in a well ventilated room as the fumes are most unpleasant.

1. Make sure the china is clean by wiping over with thinners or alcohol. Or, as mentioned before, some people prefer turps.

2. Try to use the lustre from the bottle as this is less wasteful than using a dish.

3. Dip brush into bottle. Press against side to remove surplus and apply what remains.

4. For large surfaces, it is probably better to 'pad'. To do this paint on the lustre with a soft brush and quickly add lavender oil. This will help a little, although you still have to work fast. Even if brushed on, the additional medium will do no harm but will help the brush marks to melt together. (Blotches can be caused by lavender oil in dark lustres).

5. Padding will lighten the colour but a further tint will help strengthen it. Fire after each application.

6. Do not leave the cap off the lustre bottle as it will thicken. Lustres are very sensitive and easily contaminated, it is not necessary to have a different brush for each colour but you must make sure the brush is very clean. Always keep bottles away from sunlight and in an upright position.

7. Do not get confused with lustre essence and lustre thinners. Lustre essence is far superior to thinner, it is based on special oils not only to help thin down a lustre but also to aid the application and the brilliancy of the colour. Thinner is purely for thinning down a lustre and the more you add the weaker the lustre becomes. Lustre essence is used to condition the brush before putting the brush into the lustre.

8. Most lustre will survive many firings but lustres such as red and purple may start to fade after a couple of fires. Often orange lustre will just rub off after having been fired. This can be overcome by coating orange with Mother or Pearl or Yellow Lustre on the next fire.

9. Mother of Pearl lustre will often change or distort other lustre if it is put on at the same time as other lustres. Sometimes if it is applied over another fired lustre it will change the colour of the original lustre.

Grounding

Grounding is the method used to achieve a solid colour on a piece of china e.g. the border plate on page 35. Some colours will work better for grounding than others. If you are attending a class ask your teacher for advice, if not it is best to test fire some colours first. Should the first coat not cover the china as well as you would like it to, then repeat the process for a better covering.

'Wet Grounding' or 'Tinting'

When you decide to do grounding - it is probably better to work on a few pieces at once, as the pieces need a little higher firing than usual.

Decide on the pieces of china you wish to 'ground or tint', clean them thoroughly with alcohol or methylated spirits. Choose the colour you are going to use and place your dry colour onto your mixing tile. Add enough fat oil to bind the dry colour together.

You can make your own fat oil by leaving the lid off of a jar of 'real' turpentine and placing the jar in a warm place. Eventually the liquid will evaporate away and leave 'fat oil' in the bottom of the jar. What is left will look like golden syrup - or maple syrup. This may take about one month.

When your dry colour and fat oil have been mixed together well, add turps. to the mixture; a little at a time. Your aim is to make the mixture as runny as open medium, it will run off the palette knife. Just as the mixture is beginning to work add a drop of aniseed oil to help keep it open. If the mix starts to dry whilst you are applying it to your china then add more turps to keep it runny. When you think the mixture is alright, use a large brush to apply it to your china; this is useful for the rims around plates. When you have covered the area required, use a fine sponge or a silk pad and work quickly to 'pounce' the colour to an even coat.

The result is best when thin coats of colour are used. After the first coat fire 820 °C, cone 015. Repeat the application of colour and fire again.

Dry Grounding

Any time you are going to work with excess powder paint, please wear a mask over your nose and mouth; lightweight masks are available from chemists in the UK.

You will need: Your pieces of china that you have decided to 'ground' - clean them thoroughly and do not touch the surface being ground with your fingers after it has been cleaned.

Grounding oil - This is a very thick oil to which we add pure turps. to 'thin' it down. Some countries now sell grounding oil ready to use.

Pure turps, palette knife, clean tile, a fairly wide old nylon artists brush to spread the oil with, a silk pounce. The silk pounce is made by covering a ball of cotton wool with two layers of fine silk, the silk is held in place with an elastic band.

A large sheet of newspaper and the powder paint you have chosen as your grounding colour.

Before you start to groundlay, you may wish to 'mask' off areas of your china. There are masking fluids available at your china shops, or there are masking fluids available at hobby shops that work well. Apply the masking fluid and let it dry thoroughly. If you are using the thick grounding oil you need to get it to the right consistency. Place a small amount of oil on your clean mixing tile, about enough to cover a one inch circle. Add about three drops of pure turpentine and mix them thoroughly together with your palette knife. The aim is for the mixture to run smoothly from your palette knife. You may need a few more drops of turpentine and when it is just about right, add a couple of drops of a good copaiba oil and mix thoroughly. You are going to brush this oil mixture onto the piece of china where you want the 'ground' to be, so if you add a little of the dry china paint colour you are going to use, to the mix, you will be able to see exactly where you have brushed it on.

Quickly apply the grounding oil, thinly, with your old nylon brush, to the area you are going to ground. Next, use your silk pounce to pad out the oil. Don't be frightened, really work at padding out the oil. If the silk becomes soaked with oil, move the silk around on the pounce by undoing the elastic band. It will take some time to get the oil even.

Next, remove any resist you have used. Place a sheet of newspaper or paper, underneath the plate. Pour the dry china paint onto the 'oiled' area of the china; you will use less colour than you think and any dry powder left can be re-used.

Taking a clean piece of cotton wool, or a large blender brush if you prefer, 'push' the dry paint very carefully over the oiled area. Do not let the cotton wool touch the oiled area. When you have covered all the oiled area with paint, the surface will have a lovely suede like finish. Be extremely careful not to catch this area with your finger nails as it 'cannot' be repaired.

To remove the excess paint, stand the plate on edge, on the piece of paper and gently tap the plate; the excess paint should fall onto the paper. For any stubborn areas, the excess paint can be removed with clean cotton wool, gently and carefully. The unused powder paint can be placed in a jar for the next time you are 'grounding'. Make sure you clean any unwanted paint from the white china; don't forget the bottom of the plate or china. If the piece looks oily or you have damaged the surface, it would be better to take off all the paint and oil and start again.

Or, if you leave the piece to dry thoroughly you could then use it for sgraffito. Once the surface has dried, it is very hard and a needle or stylus will scratch out a design on the unfired piece. You can adjust your mistakes to fit your design.

Fire slowly to 820 ºC, cone 015.

Bone china usually accepts grounding very well, with porcelain do be careful not to have the colour too thick or the ground may chip off once it is fired.

If you do not get the coat of oil even, the finished colour may end up blotchy but you can give the piece a second coat of grounding.

The sign reads:

LOAF COTTAGE
MOST DIZIRABLE
FAMLY REZIDENS

Celia Shute.

Your New Home

First fire: Use penwork to establish the outlines.
Second fire: Use colours from your palette to colour the design. Names, dates etc. could be added to the design to personalise the plate.